E-A-G-L-E-S!

THE TEAM THAT FINALLY GAVE PHILLY ITS SUPER ENDING

The Philadelphia Inquirer

ACKNOWLEDGMENTS

This book would not be possible without the support and contributions of many talented people at Philadelphia Media Network.

BOOK EDITORS

Pat McLoone, Managing Editor, Sports
Gary Potosky, Sports Editor
Stephen Glynn, Deputy ME, Sunday
Jim Swan, Sports Print Coordinator
Brian Leighton, Deputy ME, Editing/Standards
Gary Miles, Assistant Sports Editor

PHOTO EDITORS

Michael Mercanti, Director of Photography
Frank Wiese, Visuals Editor

PHOTOGRAPHERS

Yong Kim, David Maialetti, Clem Murray, Michael Bryant,
Tim Tai, Elizabeth Robertson, Tom Gralish, Jessica Griffin,
Steven M. Falk, David Swanson, Jose F. Moreno, Charles Fox,
Alejandro A. Alvarez, Joseph Kaczmarek, Mark C. Psoras

EAGLES COVERAGE TEAM

Zach Berman, Les Bowen, Paul Domowitch, Jeff McLane

SPORTS COLUMNISTS

Bob Ford, Marcus Hayes, David Murphy, Mike Sielski

SPECIAL THANKS

Terrance C.Z. Egger, Publisher and CEO
Stan Wischnowski, Executive Editor, Senior VP
Gabriel Escobar, Editor, VP
Matt Broad, Marketing Director
Elizabeth Parks, Marketing Specialist

FOREWORD

BY BOB FORD / STAFF COLUMNIST

For fans of the Philadelphia Eagles, it always seemed that no football season ever held as much tantalizing promise as the next one, or as much frustration and heartache as the current one.

To be honest, the 2017 season didn't look much different while it was taking place. For it to end in the most improbable fashion, with a Super Bowl LII win over the hated New England Patriots, wasn't just the end of an NFL championship drought that had lasted 57 years. It was the beginning of a civic celebration that bonded the city from the Bell to the burbs and back again.

The victory parade went literally and figuratively through the heart of Philadelphia and will never leave.

Getting to the Super Bowl was a test of the team's resolve almost from the moment it began. The Eagles lost starters Darren Sproles, Jordan Hicks and Jason Peters to injury. They kept going. They clinched their division on a warm afternoon in Los Angeles, but also lost their MVP candidate, quarterback Carson Wentz, to a torn knee ligament. They still kept going, this time with Nick Foles, a prodigal son of the franchise, ready to replace him.

Through finishing off a 13-3 season to earn home-field advantage in the playoffs, to postseason wins over Atlanta (by a hair) and Minnesota (by a full head of it), and all the way to U.S. Bank Stadium in Minneapolis for their real moment of truth in the Super Bowl, that was quite a ride. It turned out to be an unforgettable moment, didn't it?

The story of how the Lombardi Trophy was finally brought back to Philadelphia is one for the ages. We enjoyed telling all those tales along the way and are proud to share them here with you.

OPPOSITE: The champions rejoice: Mychal Kendricks (left) starts the celebration with fellow linebacker Kamu Grugier-Hill after the Eagles finished off the New England Patriots, 41-33, in Super Bowl LII. *Tim Tai / Staff Photographer*

TABLE OF CONTENTS

OPPOSITE: Raise the woof! Eagles fan Wayne Darrow of Mickleton, N.J., gets into the team's underdog spirit during the NFC championship game against Minnesota at Lincoln Financial Field. The Eagles destroyed the Vikings, 38-7. *Elizabeth Robertson / Staff Photographer*

ON THE FRONT COVER: Eagles quarterback Nick Foles holds the Lombardi Trophy after his MVP effort in Super Bowl LII. *Tim Tai / Staff Photographer*

ON THE FRONT FLAP: The parade for the Super Bowl champions passes in front of City Hall. *Jessica Griffin / Staff Photographer*

ON THE BACK COVER: (Top) Grateful Eagles fans show their colors on Eakins Oval as the Super Bowl champions take a bow at the Art Museum. *Tim Tai / Staff Photographer* (Bottom) In an impassioned speech on the Art Museum steps, Eagles center Jason Kelce brings a Mummers feel to the festivities. Eagles rookie Sidney Jones (right) enjoys the show. *David Maialetti / Staff Photographer*

ON THE BACK FLAP: An Eagles flag waves in the crowd at the Art Museum during the team's championship celebration. *Tim Tai / Staff Photographer*

OFF TO A SPLASHY START

BY ZACH BERMAN / STAFF WRITER

LANDOVER, Md. — It's uncommon for a Week 1 victory to be celebrated by dousing a second-year head coach in Gatorade. But coach Doug Pederson's wet pullover after the Eagles' 30-17 win over the Washington Redskins demonstrated just how significant the Eagles viewed their season-opening victory over a menacing division foe, a game that had loomed over each decision and practice since the team started training camp in July.

The Eagles used a swarming defense to halt a five-game losing streak to Washington and win their first road game since last September.

The game-clinching play came in the final two minutes, when star defensive tackle Fletcher Cox scooped a dribbling fumble and ran 20 yards into the end zone.

Brandon Graham caused the fumble when he knocked the ball out of Kirk Cousins' grasp while the Redskins tried to engineer a fourth-quarter comeback from a 22-17 deficit. The officials reviewed the play to determine whether it was a fumble or an incomplete pass, and referee Brad Allen said after the game that "there was nothing conclusive that would overturn the ruling on the field," which was that Cousins' empty hand went forward.

Cox finished with a sack, a forced fumble, a fumble recovery, and a touchdown. Graham added two sacks and Tim Jernigan another. Jordan Hicks recovered a fumble and Jalen Mills made his first career interception. Overall, the defense limited Washington to only 264 yards and a 3-of-11 effort on third downs. The bad news

was that top cornerback Ronald Darby was carted off the field with an ankle injury.

"I think the defense has to lead this team in order for this team to be good," Cox said. "It starts with the guys up front. The guys up front have to step up and play a big role if this team is going to be really good."

Quarterback Carson Wentz went 26 of 39 for 307 yards with two touchdowns and one interception.

The offense's highlight came on the third play of the game. Wentz eluded two defenders, set his feet, and hurled a deep pass to Nelson Agholor, who hauled in the ball at the 18-yard line, broke a tackle, and ran the rest of the way to give the Eagles a 7-0 lead.

Wentz's afternoon wasn't unblemished. He was charged with a fumble after a short

OPPOSITE: Quarterback Carson Wentz pauses in the tunnel at FedEx Field before the Eagles open the season against the Redskins. *David Maialetti / Staff Photographer*

RIGHT: Redskins linebacker Mason Foster soars by on a missed tackle, but Carson Wentz keeps his eyes downfield.

Yong Kim / Staff Photographer

pass to Agholor sailed over Agholor's head and turned into a lateral that the Redskins recovered. The fumble halted a potential Eagles score. Wentz also threw an interception that was returned for a touchdown on a deflected pass.

After Washington took a 14-13 lead late in the second quarter, a key sequence occurred when the Eagles drove downfield for a field goal and opened the second half with another to build a 19-14 lead.

And when the Skins threatened in the fourth quarter, Mills intercepted Cousins in the end zone to stop Washington's best chance of taking a late lead.

INQUIRER SPORTS PAGE

LEFT: Eagles wide receiver Nelson Agholor celebrates his 58-yard TD reception with Torrey Smith (82).

Clem Murray / Staff Photographer

RIGHT: Eagles Chris Long (left) and Malcolm Jenkins wrap up the Redskins' Kirk Cousins.
Yong Kim / Staff Photographer

OPPOSITE: Carson Wentz scrambles away from the Redskins' Zach Brown during the fourth quarter. Wentz passed for 307 yards in the opener.
David Maialetti / Staff Photographer

"It starts with the guys up front. The guys up front have to step up and play a big role if this team is going to be really good. "

— FLETCHER COX

ABOVE: Eagles coach Doug Pederson hugs his wife, Jeannie, after the victory at FedEx Field. *Yong Kim / Staff Photographer*

LEFT: In a rarity, Pederson gets a Gatorade shower from his players after an opening-day win. *David Maialetti / Staff Photographer*

OPPOSITE: Fletcher Cox picks up a fumble by Washington quarterback Kirk Cousins and heads past Morgan Moses (76) for the end zone. *Yong Kim / Staff Photographer*

A LOSS, BUT MANY GAINS

BY DAVID MURPHY / COLUMNIST

KANSAS CITY, Mo. — Right now, the Eagles are a good football team. There's your big takeaway. Metaphorically, at least.

It's easy to dwell on the negative after a loss like the 27-20 defeat they suffered to the Chiefs. Like, for instance, the actual takeaways. Carson Wentz was asked twice what happened on the turnover that tilted the game for good, and both times his tone told you more than his words.

He made the kind of mistake that a human being will often make when confronted with a situation he has never before experienced. In this case, it was a screen pass that was dead on arrival, his intended receiver lost in a moving pile of bodies, the pass rush bearing down. He made a panicky throw and did not execute it particularly well, and from there transpired the outcome the Eagles could least afford. The ball bounced off a red helmet, into the arms of a red jersey, and, just like that, the probabilities turned.

"I was more or less just trying to throw it away," Wentz said.

But a mistake doesn't become a problem until it happens again, and Wentz's tone suggested it won't. Once you take that into consideration, there isn't much about the Eagles' performance that suggests they don't currently reside at the extreme positive end of the spectrum of where they possibly could be heading into Week 3.

No, they can't run the ball. We already knew that, though. They're perilously thin in the secondary. But, again, how is that new? If anything, the first couple of weeks have sown some doubt about whether we accurately estimated the potential impact of their two biggest Achilles' heels. The secondary, in particular, has been a revelation. Maybe not of its own accord . . . Turns out, it's a lot easier to cover receivers downfield when the quarterback is forced to give up on them before they're ready. Through two games, the Eagles' front four has been as advertised, especially the two guys in the middle. Tim Jernigan looks to be playing even better than the Eagles' most optimistic hopes. Fletcher Cox is Fletcher Cox. For the majority of this game, four of the Eagles' five defensive backs in their nickel scheme were guys making a combined $3.5 million this season. One was a rookie playing in his first game.

The Eagles' pass rush started strong last year. This year, though, their performances

---

OPPOSITE: Chiefs coach Andy Reid talks to an old friend, Eagles coach Doug Pederson, after Kansas City's win. *David Maialetti / Staff Photographer*

RIGHT: Eagles running back Darren Sproles fumbles the ball against the Chiefs.
David Maialetti / Staff Photographer

have come against two of the better offensive lines in the National Football League. They sacked Alex Smith four times and pressured him numerous others. Jim Schwartz's blitz and coverage schemes left the veteran game manager visibly confused on several occasions. Maybe that won't always be the case. Things change fast in the National Football League. They say a coach doesn't even know his team until October. The Eagles started 3-0 last year.

Still, the Eagles looked like a better team in this loss to the Chiefs than they did in last year's wins over the Browns and the Bears.

LEFT: Tight end Zach Ertz catches a deflected pass in front of the Chiefs' Eric Murray. Ertz caught five passes for 97 yards. *David Maialetti / Staff Photographer*

ABOVE: Eagles center Jason Kelce gets a kiss from his brother, Chiefs tight end Travis Kelce, after the game.
David Maialetti / Staff Photographer

LEFT: Chiefs cornerback Eric Murray knocks the ball away from Eagles receiver Alshon Jeffery on a long pass to the end zone to end the game. *Yong Kim / Staff Photographer*

OPPOSITE: Chiefs safety Daniel Sorensen flies over halfback Darren Sproles to hit Carson Wentz in the fourth quarter.
David Maialetti / Staff Photographer

BIG KICK SLAYS GIANTS

BY JEFF MCLANE / STAFF WRITER

Jake Elliott has a one-minute rule.

"If you miss a kick you've got one minute to get over it and bounce back," Elliott said. "You make a kick and you've got one minute to enjoy it."

Rules are made to be broken. Elliott, the Eagles kicker for not even two weeks, can be excused if he basks in the afterglow of his game-winning, last-second, 61-yard field goal for more than just 60 seconds.

"We'll give it a day," he said. "24 hours."

It may take more than a day for players and fans to come down from the high of the Eagles' gutsy 27-24 home win over the New York Giants. But for kickers like Elliott, who has already bounced around the NFL and had to rebound from two misses in just his two lone career games, maintaining an even keel is almost a must.

"It's a little surreal. It's the life of a kicker, though," Elliott said. "You have your ultimate ups and ultimate downs. "

Just a quarter earlier it looked as if maybe Elliott, who was signed only after Caleb Sturgis suffered a hip injury, could be in jeopardy of losing his job. He hooked a 52-yard attempt wide left, which is a difficult distance for any kicker, but coming a week after he had hooked a 30-yard try, there were no guarantees.

But as he did last week when he drained a 40-yarder, Elliott bounced back and connected on a 46-yarder to tie the score, 24-24, with 56 seconds left, and then, just 55 ticks later, drilled the longest field goal in Eagles history.

Elliott's previous career long of 56 yards occurred four years ago, when he was a freshman at Memphis. And he had kicked other 50-plus-yard field goals in college. But 61 yards? Elliott hadn't even tried from that distance in practice over the last two weeks.

But distance has never been a problem for the 5-foot-7, 165-pound Elliott. His 52-yard boot would have been good from 60-plus yards had he been straight. And Eagles coach Doug Pederson said that Elliott's booming kickoffs were part of the conversation as he and special-teams coach Dave Fipp mulled whether to give the 61-yarder a go.

"I definitely ran over there real wide-eyed wanting to get it done," Elliott said.

But the decision wasn't made immediately, and when a timeout was called before the kick, Elliott said, he wasn't even sure

OPPOSITE: Jake Elliott exults after his 61-yard field goal at the finish lifted the Eagles past the Giants. *Clem Murray / Staff Photographer*

which team had called for it because the play clock was ticking down. The Giants' decision to ice the kicker actually may have backfired.

"We weren't all that set," Elliott said, "so it was kind of good to regroup there and not be too rushed."

It gave Elliott the opportunity to run back to the sideline and practice another kick into the net.

"I wanted to make it feel as in-game of the flow as possible," Elliott said.

Long-snapper Rick Lovato's snap and Donnie Jones' hold were clean and Elliott powered through the football.

"If you miss a kick you've got one minute to get over it and bounce back."

— JAKE ELLIOTT

LEFT: Giants safety Darian Thompson tackles Darren Sproles on what turned out to be his last play of the season. Sproles suffered a torn left knee ligament and a broken right forearm. *Clem Murray / Staff Photographer*

OPPOSITE: Eagles owner Jeffrey Lurie joins defensive end Brandon Graham (55) and safety Malcolm Jenkins during the national anthem. Jenkins raises his fist as a form of protest. *Yong Kim / Staff Photographer*

ABOVE: Corey Clement prepares to land in the end zone on a 15-yard scoring run in the fourth quarter.

Yong Kim / Staff Photographer

RIGHT: Running back LeGarrette Blount is congratulated by his position coach, Duce Staley, and head coach Doug Pederson after his 1-yard touchdown run.

Clem Murray / Staff Photographer

Carson Wentz scrambles away from New York's Jason Pierre-Paul (90) and Robert Thomas to pick up a first down. *Clem Murray / Staff Photographer*

OPPOSITE: Giants quarterback Eli Manning reacts after a tackle by Vinny Curry. Manning threw two interceptions. *Clem Murray / Staff Photographer*

LEFT: Eagles kicker Jake Elliott is carried off the field by Kamu Grugier-Hill (left) and Mychal Kendricks after his 61-yard field goal beat the Giants.
Clem Murray / Staff Photographer

TAKING OVER OUT WEST

BY ZACH BERMAN / STAFF WRITER

CARSON, Calif. — It didn't matter that the Eagles were nearly 3,000 miles from Philadelphia. From the start to the end of their 26-24 win over the Los Angeles Chargers, it sounded as if they were playing on South Broad Street.

And when the Eagles ran out the clock on the final six-plus minutes of the victory, the traveling and transplanted fans joined to chant "Let's go, Eagles!" and offered cheers that seemed to come from most of the 25,374 in attendance. Eagles veterans who have become used to a vocal road contingent admitted they have never seen a road crowd as disproportionately in favor of the visiting team as the one at the StubHub Center. Younger players are realizing that they could fly five hours and still experience a home-field advantage.

Games like Sunday's will only elevate the excitement among Eagles fans. The Eagles improved to 3-1, taking first place in the NFC East and appearing to be a contender in the conference. A team that couldn't win close games or on the road last season has won two games away from home in back-to-back weeks by a combined five points.

"They're learning from last year, learning from this year," coach Doug Pederson said. "They're coming together. That's exciting. It's fun to watch."

Two weeks ago, Pederson defended his seldom use of the running game. Against Los Angeles, the Eagles rushed for 214 yards. LeGarrette Blount was the star, rushing 16 times for 136 yards. Wendell Smallwood added a rushing touchdown.

The running backs were at their best in the fourth quarter. After the Chargers cut the score to 19-17 with 13 minutes, 42 seconds remaining, the Eagles' lead could have been in danger. They needed a response. And that response was the 250-pound Blount.

Blount burst through the Chargers line on the second play of the drive, and he welcomed anyone who dared to cross his path. He broke four tackles and carried the ball 68 yards before the Chargers could drag him down. It was a demoralizing run for the Chargers, and it was the very reason the Eagles signed Blount in May to be their power rusher.

They didn't have as much success when they neared the goal line, and they needed a Chargers penalty to bail them out and offer a fresh set of downs. The Eagles didn't

---

OPPOSITE: Wide receiver Alshon Jeffery scores the game's first touchdown on an 8-yard pass from Carson Wentz. Korey Toomer (left), Trevor Williams (center) and Tre Boston can't stop him. *Yong Kim / Staff Photographer*

RIGHT: Chris Long hits Chargers quarterback Philip Rivers and forces a first-quarter fumble. Derek Barnett recovered it for the Eagles. *Yong Kim / Staff Photographer*

OPPOSITE: Eagles fans at the StubHub Center rejoice after Alshon Jeffery's first-quarter touchdown. *Yong Kim / Staff Photographer*

spoil that chance, with Smallwood jumping into the end zone to give them a 26-17 lead.

The defense couldn't hold that advantage. Chargers quarterback Philip Rivers found Keenan Allen across the middle for a 50-yard catch on third down, and then hit Hunter Henry in the back of the end zone to make it a two-point game again with 6 minutes, 44 seconds remaining.

Carson Wentz and the offense returned to the field and they never left. By the time the two-minute warning hit, the players looked around the huddle and said one more first down would clinch the game. That's when Blount rushed for his final 15 yards.

ABOVE: Eagles cornerback Rasul Douglas prevents Keenan Allen from making a catch in the end zone.
Yong Kim / Staff Photographer

RIGHT: Chargers safety Tre Boston goes low in an effort to stop the bruising LeGarrette Blount.
Yong Kim / Staff Photographer

LEFT: Tight end Zach Ertz gets a step on Chargers linebacker Jatavis Brown and pulls in a pass.

Yong Kim / Staff Photographer

WHAT A COMEBACK ROUTE

BY MIKE SIELSKI / COLUMNIST

Before and after the Eagles' organized team activities last spring, Nelson Agholor retreated to his hometown for a series of training sessions with an old friend and mentor that would anneal his mind as much as his body.

The hardest year of his football life — a sexual-assault allegation, a mistake-filled season, a mini-meltdown in Seattle, the weight of unfulfilled expectations for a first-round draft pick — had ended. He needed to wash it all away, feel clean again. He flew down to Tampa, Fla., to work again with former NFL wide receiver Yo Murphy, and the conditioning drills that Murphy put him through had a dual purpose. Yes, Agholor wanted to be faster and stronger, but the intangible benefits that those improvements brought meant as much to him, if not more. All those dropped passes last season were preying on his psyche, causing his mental errors to multiply and his confidence to plummet, and the solution was to make himself physically better, to trust that his eyes and hands and legs and feet were enough for him to thrive at football's highest level.

"I don't think you take a step back from your hard work," Murphy said in a phone interview, hours after Agholor caught four passes for 93 yards, including a 72-yard touchdown, in the Eagles' 34-7 rout of the visiting Cardinals. "You take a step back about how you are wired for the moment. It's more about pushing your chips all in. 'I did the work. Now it's time to just play.' "

"He's wound tight. He's a very analytical guy. He sometimes has to know that, even though he's a smart guy, his athletic ability needs to be his prime mover, not his brain."

It sounds counterintuitive, that a player whose greatest problem was that he was trying too hard would right himself by trying even harder. But for all the freedom and self-assurance that Agholor is displaying now — and that backward splashdown into the end zone on his touchdown was nothing if not the celebratory act of a

---

OPPOSITE: Just dropping in, Nelson Agholor falls into the end zone after his 72-yard pass reception. *Clem Murray / Staff Photographer*

> **"I don't think you take a step back from your hard work."**
>
> — YO MURPHY,
> NELSON AGHOLOR'S TRAINER

self-assured man — he couldn't simply relax and know that everything would fall into place for him.

After averaging a meager 11 yards per reception and catching just 59 passes and three touchdowns through his first two NFL seasons, Agholor already has 16 receptions this season and leads the Eagles'

wide receivers in yards per catch (16.6) and touchdowns (three). Like the stunning touchdown he scored against Arizona — when he sprinted past safety Budda Baker, fingertip-caught a long Carson Wentz pass, and muscled past Baker along the sideline — that kind of jump in production doesn't happen without a significant enhancement

in a receiver's pure physical attributes.

Agholor got faster and stronger, so it's easier for him to make difficult plays. And because it's easier for him to make those plays, he makes more of those plays. And because he does, his confidence grows, until it's all a wondrous cycle perpetuating itself.

"Speed is something that puts people off

RUSHING YARDS

122
PHILADELPHIA

31
ARIZONA

LEFT: Tight end Zach Ertz stretches over the goal line for an 11-yard touchdown reception as Arizona's tacklers come up short.
Clem Murray / Staff Photographer

OPPOSITE: The old ball game: Eagles wide receiver Torrey Smith touches off a unique end-zone celebration with (from left) Zach Ertz, Alshon Jeffrey and Carson Wentz after scoring on a 59-yard pass play.
Clem Murray / Staff Photographer

balance, and when you match that with technique, you get yourself separation," he said. "When you're not on time, you end up catching the ball in awkward positions. When you get there on time, it's easier to get in front of the football and bring it in. At the end of the day, I'm not perfect yet, and I keep on working on these things."

"I see this kid every single day, the way he walks into the building with confidence," Eagles head coach Doug Pederson said. "Nothing gets him down. He works extremely hard, and he's playing at a high level right now."

He caught that pass from Wentz in the third quarter, left Baker lying on the ground behind him, then stopped at the goal line. He turned his back to the end zone and threw his arms in the air in a V, the sound of 69,596 people rising around him. Later, someone asked him what he was thinking in that moment. "Nothing," he said. Finally, Nelson Agholor had learned to let go.

RIGHT: Eagles defensive end Vinny Curry celebrates after his sack of Carson Palmer.

David Maialetti / Staff Photographer

OPPOSITE: Eagles running back LeGarrette Blount busts through the Arizona defense.

Clem Murray / Staff Photographer

LEFT: Defensive end Vinny Curry talks with Eagles fans after the rout at Lincoln Financial Field.
Clem Murray / Staff Photographer

OPPOSITE: Eagles receiver Nelson Agholor (left) celebrates his 72-yard touchdown reception with LeGarrette Blount as Carson Wentz joins in. *Yong Kim / Staff Photographer*

THE BEAUTIFUL GAME

BY MARCUS HAYES / COLUMNIST

CHARLOTTE, N.C. — What gorgeous football.

What passionate, breathtaking, completely enjoyable football happened in Charlotte. Stars starred. Everything mattered.

The Eagles won, 28-23, and moved to 5-1. They won on the road, without right tackle Lane Johnson, on a short week, in prime time. They could — should? — be considered the best team in the NFC in this young 2017 season, all apologies to the Packers and Falcons. The Panthers had a chance at entering that argument but they fell to 4-2.

If they get a little healthier, either team has the horses to wind up in Minneapolis on Feb. 4 but, of course, not both.

Rarely does a marquee game rise to the level of its hype. Such a game should be savored.

The coaches called on their offenses and defenses to execute intricately. They did so.

The star quarterbacks made thrilling plays. The top targets made incredible catches.

And the Eagles won.

"We showed them that we are one of the top teams. That was our goal," said linebacker Nigel Bradham, the best player on the field Thursday night. "Everybody was high on this game. We came ready."

Ready for anything, which is how you beat the Panthers and Cam Newton.

"Two 4-1 teams, to come in and play that way ... short week ..." said cornerback Jalen Mills, who sealed the win with an interception. "This is a great team win."

QB Carson Wentz and tight end Zach Ertz turned two interceptions of Newton into two touchdown passes.

Near the end of the third quarter, with a defender clinging to his knees, Wentz found rookie Mack Hollins for 20 yards on third-and-16, then hit Alshon Jeffery for 37 more, the bulk of his 71 yards on four catches. And then, as the fourth quarter began, Wentz hit Nelson Agholor for the 24-yard touchdown that made it 28-16, enough for the win. Wentz finished 16-for-30 for 222 yards and three TDs.

Fletcher Cox, the Eagles' $102 million defensive tackle, returned from a two-game absence and forced an interception in the second quarter. He added a sack in the third and batted down a pass. Cox spent more time in Newton's lap than his kids.

For a few hours, football was all that mattered — the game, and the beautiful endeavor it can be.

The league should be so lucky to have it happen like this again.

OPPOSITE: Jonathan Stewart of the Panthers is gang-tackled by Eagles Mychal Kendricks (95), Nigel Bradham and Derek Barnett (96). *Yong Kim / Staff Photographer*

INQUIRER SPORTS PAGE

RIGHT: Eagles cornerback Rasul Douglas returns his interception of a Cam Newton pass 7 yards in the second quarter. *Yong Kim / Staff Photographer*

Eagles cornerback Jalen Mills stops Carolina's Kelvin Benjamin short of a first down in the second quarter. *Clem Murray / Staff Photographer*

ABOVE: Zach Ertz gets past Panthers cornerback Daryl Worley for one of his two touchdown catches. *Clem Murray / Staff Photographer*

RIGHT: Nelson Agholor scores on a 24-yard pass from Carson Wentz in the fourth quarter in Charlotte. *Clem Murray / Staff Photographer*

OPPOSITE: Panthers quarterback Cam Newton congratulates Carson Wentz after the Eagles' victory. Newton threw three interceptions. *Clem Murray / Staff Photographer*

FRANCHISE QB EMERGES

BY LES BOWEN / STAFF WRITER

Eight plays after he watched Jason Peters, the anchor of his offensive line, ride into the tunnel on a cart with a right knee injury, Carson Wentz stepped out of the clutches of Washington defensive lineman Terrell McClain and into even bigger trouble.

Redskins linebacker Mason Foster grabbed Wentz around the waist. Another defender weighed him down from the other side. Wentz's head and passing arm emerged from the scrum, long enough for him to fling the ball toward the end zone.

Somehow, Wentz saw rookie running back Corey Clement at the right sideline. And somehow Clement, who had caught exactly one previous NFL pass, timed his leap perfectly and got both feet down in-bounds, in the end zone.

It was a 9-yard touchdown pass that gave the Eagles a 24-10 lead with 5 minutes, 17 seconds remaining in the third quarter of their eventual 34-24 NFC East victory, and it was a defining moment for the team's second-year QB.

Doug Pederson called the pass "one of the best plays I've seen in a long, long time. Two young guys making that type of a play on this really big stage."

Clement said he was the last option. Wentz said Clement was "kind of like No. 3 in the progression."

"Surprised me," Clement said. "I didn't think he saw me."

"He made a great play," Foster said. "He stepped up in the pocket — we were all in his face — but he threw it up there and [Clement] made a good play. You have

to tip your hat to Wentz, he made a lot of big plays tonight, but that's what he's been doing all year."

Wentz and his team had gotten off to a horrible start in a penalty-plagued game that saw key players from both teams more or less continuously shuffling off the field. The Birds entered the second quarter trailing, 3-0. They took four penalties on their first three snaps, which ought to be a record, whether it is or not.

"Yeah, it was a sluggish start," Pederson said.

After the amazing TD pass to Clement, Wentz's third of the game, he was 13 for 20 for 216 yards and a 120 passer rating. After his next touchdown pass, a much more routine 10-yard end zone slant to Nelson Agholor, Wentz was 17 for 25 for 268 and a

---

OPPOSITE: Carson Wentz breaks into the clear against the Redskins. He finished with 63 yards on the ground. *Clem Murray / Staff Photographer*

126.3 passer rating. That time, by the way, Wentz changed the play at the line.

"It was a perfect call in the right situation," tight end Zach Ertz said.

At the risk of stating the obvious, this is what a franchise quarterback looks like. "He has an uncanny ability, when things break down, of still making big plays," center Jason Kelce said. "He really bailed us out a lot tonight, bailed us out on that play."

"He's doing a great job," Ertz said. "He's leading our team. He's the face of the franchise, the face of the city right now. It's an exciting time in Philadelphia."

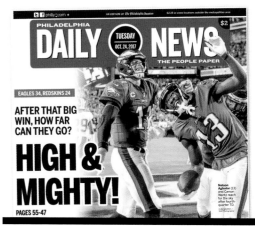

TOP LEFT: All-pro tackle Jason Peters is carted off the field after suffering a knee injury in the Redskins game. Peters missed the remainder of the season. *Clem Murray / Staff Photographer*

BOTTOM LEFT: Eagles players surround the cart carrying Peters off the field after he suffered two torn ligaments in his right knee. *Yong Kim / Staff Photographer*

OPPOSITE: Carson Wentz escapes as Eagles tackle Lane Johnson blocks Ryan Kerrigan. *Yong Kim / Staff Photographer*

8.7
PHILADELPHIA

6.1
WASHINGTON

RIGHT: Nigel Bradham drills Redskins quarterback Kirk Cousins during the first quarter. *Clem Murray / Staff Photographer*

OPPOSITE: Receiver Nelson Agholor (13) celebrates with Carson Wentz after his 10-yard TD reception gave the Eagles a 31-17 lead. *Clem Murray / Staff Photographer*

CASE FOR THE DEFENSE

BY PAUL DOMOWITCH / STAFF WRITER

Much has been made this season, and deservedly so, of the improvement by the Eagles' offense on third down.

But their defense also has been doing an impressive job of getting off the field on third down during the team's 7-1 start.

Jim Schwartz's unit went into the game against the winless 49ers ranked third in the league in third-down defense, behind only Denver and Minnesota.

It turned in another impressive third-down performance in the Birds' waterlogged 33-10 win at the Linc, allowing the Niners and their rookie quarterback, C.J. Beathard, to convert just three of 15 third-down opportunities.

Beathard completed just five of 12 third-down passes for 34 yards. Cornerback Jalen Mills intercepted Beathard on a third-and-7 play late in the first half and returned it 37 yards for a touchdown that gave the Eagles a 17-0 lead.

It was the Eagles' eighth interception of the season, six of which have come on third down. That's the most third-down interceptions in the league.

Opponents have a 47.1 passer rating on third down against the Eagles. They've completed just 54.2 percent of their third-down attempts and have converted just 23 of 45 third-down completions (51.1 percent) into first downs.

The offense came up with three touchdowns: a 12-yard run by LeGarrette Blount and TD passes from Carson Wentz to Alshon Jeffery and Zach Ertz.

Three of the six third-down interceptions have been by Mills, who this time anticipated a pass intended for Pierre Garcon.

"I've been watching film hard all week," Mills said. "Been kind of studying that route, too. I kind trusted my technique, trusted my feet and my safety over the top and jumped the route and picked the ball off."

On third down, when the Eagles have needed a stop, they've been gold. Just two of their first eight opponents have managed to convert more than 40 percent of their third-down tries against

OPPOSITE: Defensive end Vinny Curry lives it up after he stopped 49ers running back Carlos Hyde for a loss. *Clem Murray / Staff Photographer*

them — Kansas City (41.7) and the L.A. Chargers (50.0).

The Eagles' ability to stop the run also has helped. Just four of the Niners' 15 third-down situations were 3 yards or less. They threw on three of them and converted just one.

"We put a lot of emphasis, spend a lot of time on preparation, for third down during the week," safety Malcolm Jenkins said. "The ability to play the situation, whether it's third-and-short or third-and-long … It's been the calling card of this defense this year."

LEFT: Alshon Jeffery secures a catch for the Eagles above San Francisco's Ahkello Witherspoon. Jeffery caught two passes for 62 yards and a touchdown.

David Maialetti / Staff Photographer

OPPOSITE: Guard Brandon Brooks keeps San Francisco's Solomon Thomas at bay as Carson Wentz drops back to pass.

Clem Murray / Staff Photographer

ABOVE: Pick-six: Eagles cornerback Jalen Mills returns his interception of C.J. Beathard's pass 37 yards for a touchdown.
Clem Murray / Staff Photographer

LEFT: Mills gets a hug from his position coach, Cory Undlin, after his interception return for a touchdown.
Clem Murray / Staff Photographer

OPPOSITE: 49ers quarterback C.J. Beathard is decked by Fletcher Cox (top) and Chris Long after releasing a pass. It fell incomplete. *David Maialetti / Staff Photographer*

AJAYI'S A QUICK STUDY

BY MIKE SIELSKI / COLUMNIST

The Eagles officially announced the acquisition of Jay Ajayi, in a trade with the Miami Dolphins, at 8:35 a.m. on Oct. 31, and the long nights for him began soon after — after-hour study sessions with Duce Staley, the team's running backs coach. The tutorials were designed not to have Ajayi memorize the entire playbook in time for the Nov. 5 game against the Broncos, but to have him learn some simple, specific formations and calls that would be easier for him to master over just five days of preparation. Get him a few plays. Get him acclimated. Don't ask him to do too much in his debut.

Yeah … so things didn't go exactly according to plan.

"I don't think it could have been written any better than that," Ajayi said after the Eagles' 51-23 rout of the Broncos. He had rushed for 77 yards, including a stunning 46-yard sprint for a touchdown, on just eight carries. The crowd of media members who wanted to talk to him afterward reached him so quickly that he remained seated at his locker while he answered questions. He barely had room to stand even if he had wanted to.

Ajayi had arrived here amid a combination of optimism and caution. The Dolphins had traded him for a fourth-round pick, the decision couched in the cliched language that head coach Adam Gase wanted to send a message to his underachieving team. Saying goodbye to a back who rushed for 1,272 yards and eight touchdowns last season would seem an odd vessel for message-sending, and there were whispers and anonymously sourced reports out of Miami that Ajayi put his carries and statistics ahead of the team's fortunes, that he was a me-first player, that the Dolphins feared his knees wouldn't hold up over the long term.

It would seem, at least for now, that the Eagles have created an environment in which Ajayi or any player wouldn't dare be so self-centered. They are rolling at 8-1, and against Denver, the four running backs they used — Ajayi, Corey Clement, LeGarrette Blount, Wendell Smallwood — combined for 190 yards, three rushing touchdowns, and an average of 5.6 yards per carry. Early on, in fact, Ajayi helped the Eagles most by not carrying the football. Three times in the first half, Wentz relied on him as the decoy in a play-action

---

OPPOSITE: Jay Ajayi acknowledges the fans at Lincoln Financial Field after rushing for 77 yards and a touchdown in his Eagles debut. *Clem Murray / Staff Photographer*

RIGHT: Jay Ajayi dives into the end zone to punctuate his 46-yard run.
Clem Murray / Staff Photographer

or read-option fake.

Late in the second quarter, the Eagles dispensed with the decoy stuff, handing Ajayi the ball on three consecutive plays. He gained 2 yards, then gained 14 and a first down, then followed clear-out blocks from left tackle Halapoulivaati Vaitai, right guard Brandon Brooks, and center Jason Kelce around left end and through an open lane toward the end zone, diving at the left pylon and stretching out the football to break the goal line's plane for his first touchdown of the season.

His knees looked OK on that play, and he said later that they felt just fine, and if he is whole and healthy, he can make running back, once a position of uncertainty for the Eagles, one of talent and depth.

ABOVE: Eagles tight end Brent Celek emerges during pregame introductions. *Yong Kim / Staff Photographer*

LEFT: Rodney McLeod of the Eagles upends Devontae Booker on a kickoff return.

David Maialetti / Staff Photographer

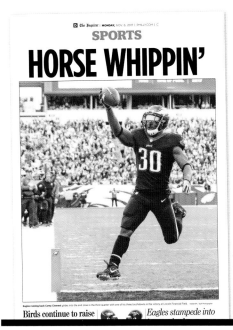

INQUIRER SPORTS PAGE

RIGHT: Eagles defensive backs Patrick Robinson (21) and Corey Graham try for an interception on a pass intended for Denver's Isaiah McKenzie. The pass was incomplete.
Yong Kim / Staff Photographer

OPPOSITE: Rookie Corey Clement leaps into the end zone on a 15-yard TD pass from Carson Wentz.
David Maialetti / Staff Photographer

RIGHT: Alshon Jeffrey catches a 4-yard pass after Carson Wentz threaded the needle between Denver's Aqib Talib and Zaire Anderson. *Clem Murray / Staff Photographer*

OPPOSITE: Carson Wentz leaves the field after his 199-yard passing performance. He threw four touchdown passes. *Clem Murray / Staff Photographer*

BELOW RIGHT: Eagles coach Doug Pederson congratulates rookie Corey Clement after his first-quarter touchdown. *Clem Murray / Staff Photographer*

BELOW: Defensive tackle Fletcher Cox pressures Denver quarterback Brock Osweiler, who threw two interceptions. *Clem Murray / Staff Photographer*

MISMATCH IN TEXAS

BY MARCUS HAYES / COLUMNIST

DALLAS — Two touchdowns vs. no touchdowns.

No interceptions vs. three interceptions.

Thirty-seven to nine.

Any questions?

The Wentz Wagon rolled into Arlington and rolled over the face of the Cowboys franchise; the reigning rookie of the year; the man who forced failed quarterback and kick holder Tony Romo to find his true calling, as a brilliant football analyst.

A prime-time national audience watched the North Dakota Kid make play after play in the Jerry Dome, where the Dak Attack led the Pokes to the playoffs a season ago.

It was a rematch, but not really. Last season, in Game 7, Carson Wentz dinked-and-dunked the Eagles to the threshold of an upset that might have saved the season,

but Prescott's fourth-quarter drive tied the game. Wentz had two chances to respond. He did not. The Eagles lost in overtime and fell to 4-3, the first of a six-game losing streak that ruined Wentz's rookie year. As for the budding rivalry, that game decided little. Neither did the meaningless rematch, the season finale, in which Prescott played only two series.

This would be the best barometer so far: two healthy, seasoned leaders on winning teams in a game that would go far in deciding the NFC East.

Decidedly: Wentz.

He finished 14 for 27 for 168 yards, the two TDs, no picks. And he was better than that. He wasn't sacked. He made few mistakes. He won. Big.

Prescott was 18 for 31 for 145 yards,

three picks, no scores. And he was worse than that. He was sacked four times. He was gun-shy and rattled. He lost. Big.

Wentz wasn't just good; he was thrillingly good.

His signature play might otherwise go overlooked, despite its breathless beauty, so let's appreciate its magnificence. It came on the Eagles' final touchdown drive, third-and-2 at the Eagles' 38. Wentz dropped back, planted, sidestepped blitzing linebacker Damien Wilson; then, with Wilson doggedly latched onto his left ankle, he flat-footed a pass 10 yards to Alshon Jeffery.

It was a magnificent play, subtly ferocious; gladiatorial. It took every iota of agility to make Wilson whiff; every ounce of Wentz's strength to turn his shoulders and torque

OPPOSITE: With Cowboys linebacker Damien Wilson grabbing his ankle, Carson Wentz completes a flat-footed pass to Alshon Jeffrey. *Clem Murray / Staff Photographer*

his body to supply the pass its velocity; every scintilla of athletic ability to put the pass in the right spot at the right moment.

Very few quarterbacks in NFL history have possessed the size, strength, arm and instinct to even have a chance to make that play. Wentz has it all.

So go ahead. Compare him to Big Ben, or Favre, or Donovan. He's worthy.

Prescott, simply, is not.

Look: Dak's good. When he's protected by the league's best line, complemented by the league's top rusher, Prescott makes the plays that need to be made.

Tasked with winning on his own merit, he does not.

Not yet, anyway. Maybe not ever.

Nobody's perfect. In this game, Wentz was much closer to perfection than Prescott.

Maybe Prescott can rebound in the rematch, again the season finale, this time on Dec. 31.

Probably not.

ABOVE: Carson Wentz fans stake their claim to a spot at the Cowboys' stadium. *Clem Murray / Staff Photographer*

LEFT: Alshon Jeffery celebrates a two-point conversion for the Eagles in front of Cowboys cornerback Anthony Brown.
Clem Murray / Staff Photographer

OPPOSITE: Eagles players are all smiles on the sideline as the clock runs out at AT&T Stadium. *Clem Murray / Staff Photographer*

LEFT: Eagles running back Kenjon Barner scores on a 4-yard run, his only carry of the game. *Clem Murray / Staff Photographer*

OPPOSITE: Patrick Robinson (21) and Trey Burton upend the Cowboys' Ryan Switzer on a first-quarter kickoff return. *David Maialetti / Staff Photographer*

RIGHT: Defensive tackle Tim Jernigan and defensive end Vinny Curry (75) get to Dak Prescott.

Dave Maialetti / Staff Photographer

OPPOSITE: Jay Ajayi outruns Datone Jones in the third quarter. Ajayi finished with 91 rushing yards.

Clem Murray / Staff Photographer

ROUTS BECOME ROUTINE

BY DAVID MURPHY / COLUMNIST

As you looked around the Eagles' locker room, you saw veteran players who have seen this kind of thing before. LeGarrette Blount lost just 10 regular-season games in his three seasons with the Patriots, a run that ended with 10 straight victories from Week 11 through the Super Bowl. Torrey Smith went 12-4 as a rookie with the Ravens and won a ring in his second NFL season. Malcolm Jenkins started his rookie season 13-0 en route to a Super Bowl victory.

That is the realm this Eagles team inhabits after a 31-3 win over the Bears. Not because the Eagles did what most reasonable minds expected against an overmatched, under-quarterbacked opponent, but because they are making a habit of doing it. Last week, it was the Cowboys. The game before, it was the Broncos, which came a week after the 49ers.

Seven times this season, the Eagles have scored at least 30 points while beating an opponent by double digits.

This is a distinctive realm the Eagles have played themselves into. Since 2009, that has happened just 13 times over the course of an entire season, with seven of them coming by way of the Patriots and Broncos.

That's an important distinction, and it starts with a word we mentioned earlier: habit. Talk to Jenkins, talk to Smith, talk to anyone in that locker room who has experienced NFL success, and they'll tell you the best teams they have seen are the ones for which success has become habitual. The state that they occupy is the NFL's equivalent of nirvana, one in which victories are not fortuitous ends but inevitable by products of each week of practice: Of course, we won. It was the only potential outcome.

The Patriots probably typify this mode of operation better than any other team. To watch them is to watch the closest approximation of a football automaton. Every block, every tackle, every angle is executed with such flawless precision that it becomes difficult to envision a scenario in which it can be stopped.

"It sounds cliche, but it's about practicing well," Smith said. "We've got great energy. We've got a lot of attention to detail. The coaches are preparing their tails off as well. It all goes together. I mean, you look at plays sometimes, and it's like game reps in practice. When you practice like that, it tends to show on Sunday."

OPPOSITE: LeGarrette Blount hurdles Chicago safety Eddie Jackson as he picks up 22 yards on a run. Blount rushed for 97 yards. *Clem Murray / Staff Photographer*

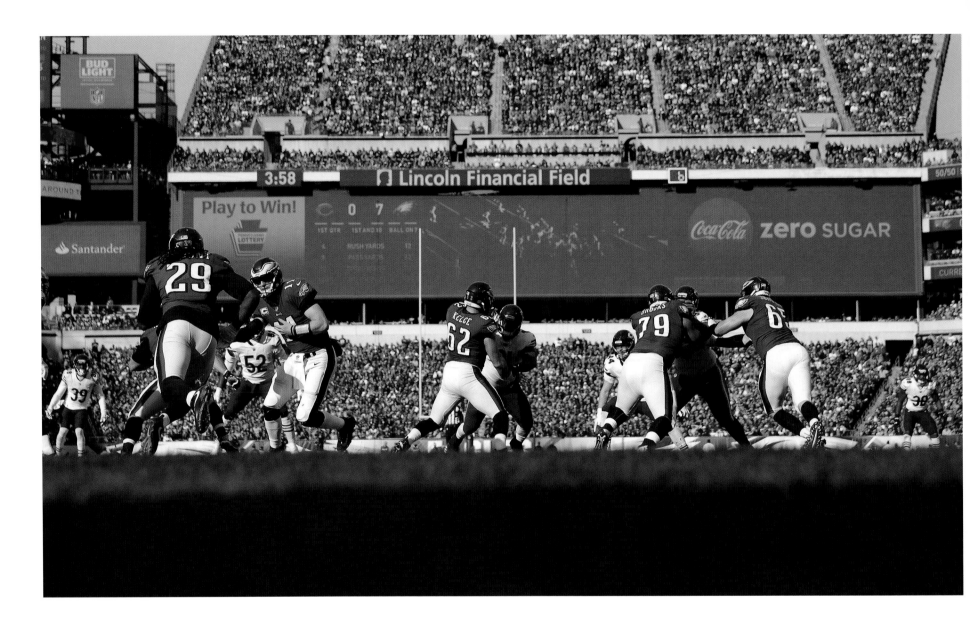

There are three constants with this team: an exquisitely designed and flawlessly executed running game, an unyielding and technically sound defense, and, of course, a quarterback who is playing with as much confidence and command as any of the more seasoned arms against whom he will square off come playoff time.

Take away any one of these three aspects and the Eagles are still a good team, but they're probably inconsistent enough to make a Sunday interesting every now and then. At the moment, though, they inhabit a realm that only the Patriots have habitually claimed in recent years, operating with a level of precision that seems far outside the bounds of normalcy for any human endeavor.

LEFT: Tight end Zach Ertz breaks a tackle by Bears linebacker Sam Acho and heads upfield. Ertz caught 10 passes for 103 yards and a touchdown. *Clem Murray / Staff Photographer*

OPPOSITE: Carson Wentz hands off the ball to LeGarrette Blount during the Eagles' lopsided win at the Linc. *David Maialetti / Staff Photographer*

DAILY NEWS FRONT PAGE

RIGHT: Defensive end Steven Means leaps to deflect a punt by the Bears' Pat O'Donnell.

Clem Murray / Staff Photographer

OPPOSITE: Switching sports in an end-zone celebration, the Eagles pretend to be bowling pins.

David Maialetti / Staff Photographer

WAKE-UP CALL IN SEATTLE

BY ZACH BERMAN / STAFF WRITER

SEATTLE — Carson Wentz came within one yard of tying the score in a 24-10 loss to the Seattle Seahawks, of pulling off the theatrics that marked what has been a magical Eagles season. But the ball was stripped from Wentz's grasp just before he reached the end zone on a third-quarter run, and Wentz jumped up in time to see the ball bounce out of bounds for a touchback.

It was that kind of night for the Eagles. One week ago, during their ninth consecutive win, they recovered their own fumble for a touchdown. Against the Seahawks, they lost possession on the defining play of the game. That was their best chance to keep pace against a desperate Seahawks team that outplayed the Eagles on the first leg of the their critical two-game road trip.

The Eagles had no answer for Seahawks quarterback Russell Wilson, who could rival Wentz in MVP conversations after a splendid performance against an Eagles defense that had been dominating foes this season.

The Eagles fell to 10-2 and headed to California for a week of practice leading to the game against the 9-3 Los Angeles Rams, trying to stay atop a competitive NFC. It's not time to jump off the Eagles bandwagon — it was probably too greedy to expect the team to finish 15-1 — but the Eagles finally showed vulnerabilities after more than two months of near-pristine football.

"Can't make those mistakes against good football teams on the road and expect to win," coach Doug Pederson said. "Just can't do it."

The Eagles learned what could happen when Wentz is not the best quarterback on the field. Wentz finished 29 of 45 for 348 yards with a touchdown, an interception and a fumble. His quarterback rating was 86.9. That was dwarfed by Wilson, who went 20 of 31 for 227 yards and three touchdowns with a 118.6 quarterback rating.

"We made too many mistakes to win against a hot quarterback," safety Malcolm Jenkins said. "He made some special plays and we knew he would."

OPPOSITE: Carson Wentz fumbles at the goal line as Earl Thomas of the Seahawks moves in. The ball went out of the end zone for a touchback.

David Maialetti / Staff Photographer

RIGHT: Carson Wentz gets a hug from Jay Ajayi late in the loss that ended the Eagles' nine-game winning streak. *David Maialetti / Staff Photographer*

OPPOSITE LEFT: Vinny Curry cannot get to Russell Wilson in time as the Seahawks QB unloads a pass. *David Maialetti / Staff Photographer*

OPPOSITE RIGHT: Seattle's Russell Wilson escapes the grasp of Brandon Graham. Wilson passed for 227 yards and three touchdowns. *Yong Kim / Staff Photographer*

Wilson was hot from the opening drive. Even though the Seahawks settled for a field goal, Wilson moved the ball against the Eagles and showed signs that the Birds were not quite playing against C.J. Beathard. He built a 10-0 lead later in the quarter when he found Jimmy Graham for an 11-yard touchdown, giving the Eagles their largest first-quarter deficit of the season.

With a chance to tie the score on the opening possession of the second half, Wentz committed his costly fumble. Before that play, the Eagles had success moving the ball on the Seahawks, including Alshon Jeffery and Zach Ertz more than in the first half. (Ertz later left the game with a concussion.) But Wentz's fumble spoiled a precious opportunity.

Wentz faked a handoff and steamed forward for the potential score before Sheldon Richardson ripped the ball out of his hands, resulting in the Eagles' first red zone turnover this season.

"I fumbled it. It happens," Wentz said. "It's tough to do that on the road in close situations like that, especially when you're down there at the 1-yard line. Tough to do that and expect to win."

Wilson converted the turnover into points. It took him 11 plays and 80 yards, with the biggest one a 47-yard pass to Doug Baldwin on a third-and-10 when the Eagles blitzed. Wilson recognized the blitz and hurled the deep pass that set up a 1-yard touchdown to Tyler Lockett for a two-touchdown lead. Good luck coming back from that deficit in Seattle.

Nelson Agholor had a career night at the site of the worst game of his career last year, finishing with seven catches for 141 yards and a score.

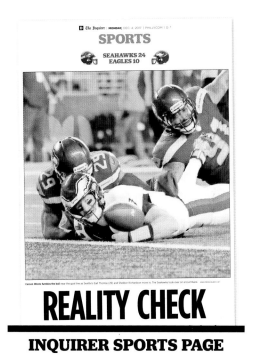

SPORTS

SEAHAWKS 24
EAGLES 10

Carson Wentz fumbles the ball near the goal line as Seattle's Earl Thomas (29) and Sheldon Richardson move in. The Seahawks took over on a touchback.

REALITY CHECK

INQUIRER SPORTS PAGE

"We made too many mistakes to win against a hot quarterback."

— MALCOLM JENKINS

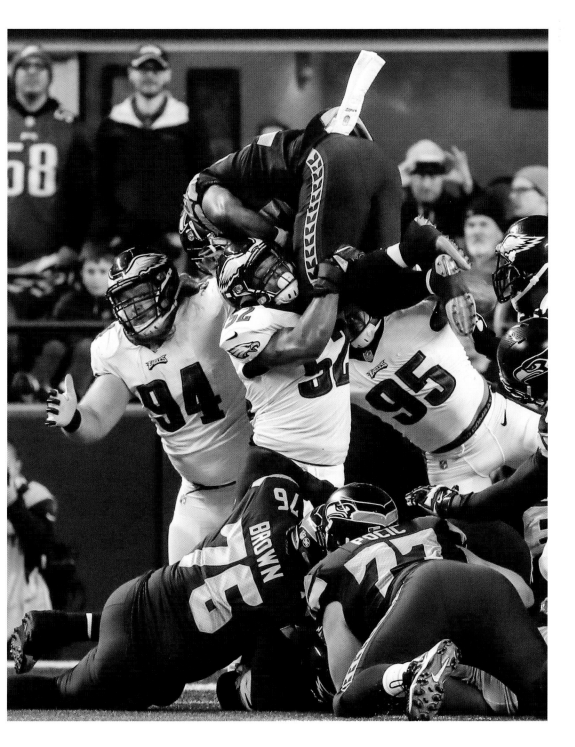

ABOVE: Nelson Agholor catches a touchdown pass for the Eagles in the midst of a huge game: seven receptions for 141 yards. *Yong Kim / Staff Photographer*

LEFT: Defensive tackle Beau Allen (left) teams up with linebackers Najee Goode (center) and Mychal Kendricks to stop Seattle's Mike Davis from taking the high road. *Yong Kim / Staff Photographer*

OPPOSITE: Carson Wentz throws the football as Seattle's Quinton Jefferson tries to bring him down. *Yong Kim / Staff Photographer*

WINCING FOR WENTZ

BY LES BOWEN / STAFF WRITER

LOS ANGELES — This was one scramble Carson Wentz could not make on his own. Wentz was seated backward on a green motorized cart, head down, texting intently. A towel partially covered his left leg, the lower portion of which was encased in a black padded brace.

As the cart roared up the Los Angeles Memorial Coliseum tunnel from the visiting locker room, reporters jogged in its wake. At the top of the tunnel, screened by guards, Wentz hopped off the cart and made his way to the Eagles' chartered bus. A pair of unidentified hands reached out to embrace him in a hug as he moved into the doorway, on the opposite side of the bus from where reporters watched from behind a fence.

Wentz wore a black 2017 NFC East Champions cap, the one handed to each player in the victorious locker room after the Eagles' 43-35 victory over the host Los Angeles Rams. It might be destined to become an ironic souvenir, like tickets to the maiden voyage of the Titanic.

Wentz is thought to have torn his left anterior cruciate ligament with 3 minutes, 53 seconds remaining in the third quarter, on a scramble on which he ended up diving into the end zone for a touchdown that didn't count, Wentz's legs sandwiched between Rams defensive lineman Morgan Fox and linebacker Mark Barron.

Wentz played four more snaps, breaking Sonny Jurgensen's franchise single-season record for touchdown passes with his 33rd of the season, his fourth of the afternoon, on a ball he might have been throwing to Nelson Agholor that went past Agholor in the end zone and was plucked adroitly by Alshon Jeffery.

That was Wentz's last touchdown pass of the season, on a day when the Eagles redefined winning the battle and losing the war.

"He didn't say anything," wide receiver Torrey Smith said when asked about those four plays. "That shows you how tough he is. I'm praying for the best for him."

On any other afternoon, the receivers would have been a major story unto themselves, the Eagles netting 333 passing yards on 29 catches against what had been the NFL's seventh-ranked pass defense. Agholor redeemed himself for a first-possession interception he caused by coming back to catch eight passes for 64 yards, including a clutch grab on third down from

---

OPPOSITE: Eagles fan Eric Glenn of Horsham reacts to the news of Carson Wentz's injury as he watches the game's telecast at XFINITY Live! in South Philadelphia.

Elizabeth Robertson / Staff Photographer

> ## "He didn't say anything. That shows you how tough he is. I'm praying for the best for him."
>
> — TORREY SMITH

backup Nick Foles to allow the Eagles to virtually run out the clock.

Smith's six catches netted 100 yards. With tight end Zach Ertz sidelined by a concussion, Trey Burton caught five passes for 71 yards and a pair of touchdowns, and Brent Celek's lone catch became his first touchdown since 2015. Jeffery's TD catch was tremendous, one of his five grabs for 52 yards.

But there was only one Eagles story on this day. Smith noted that Wentz is "probably the MVP of the league."

"He's the leader of our team, playing out of his mind," said right guard Brandon Brooks, who said he had no idea anything was wrong until after the touchdown was scored and they went to the sideline. "He was the same guy" after the play on which Wentz was injured.

"That's why he is who he is," Agholor said.

"Hopefully he's OK. If not, it's devastating," Celek said. "We've just got to go out there and play for him. I talked to him, told him I love him. We'll see what happens."

Foles did a nice job of coaxing the Birds over the finish line for the win, and he certainly is better than many other backup quarterbacks, but Carson Wentz is what makes the Eagles special. As they took those division-champion caps off for a nap on the charter home early in the morning, his teammates surely came to grips with that.

INQUIRER FRONT PAGE

LEFT: Malcolm Jenkins (27) helps Rodney McLeod along after McLeod recovered a fumble during the fourth quarter. *Yong Kim / Staff Photographer*

OPPOSITE: Carson Wentz during warm-ups for what would be his last game of the season.
Yong Kim / Staff Photographer

ABOVE: Carson Wentz is tackled by Rams Morgan Fox and Mark Barron on the fateful play that injured his knee. *Mark J. Terrill / AP*

ABOVE RIGHT: Wentz dives for the end zone, suffering a knee injury on the play. He left the game after throwing one last touchdown pass. *Mark J. Terrill / AP*

RIGHT: Sandwiched between the Rams' Morgan Fox and Mark Barron, Wentz suffers season-ending tears to two knee ligaments. *Mark J. Terrill / AP*

OPPOSITE: Wentz rubs his left knee after he was injured. He fired a touchdown pass to Alshon Jeffery before leaving the game. *Yong Kim / Staff Photographer*

RIGHT: Carson Wentz leaves the field at the Coliseum after he hurt his left knee. A torn anterior cruciate ligament ended his season. *Kelvin Kuo / AP*

BELOW: Watching the game's telecast at XFINITY Live! in South Philadelphia, Eagles fans react to the news of Carson Wentz's injury. *Elizabeth Robertson / Staff Photographer*

OPPOSITE: Pressed into service, Nick Foles passes as Rams (from left) Samson Ebukam, Alec Ogletree and Robert Quinn close in. *Yong Kim / Staff Photographer*

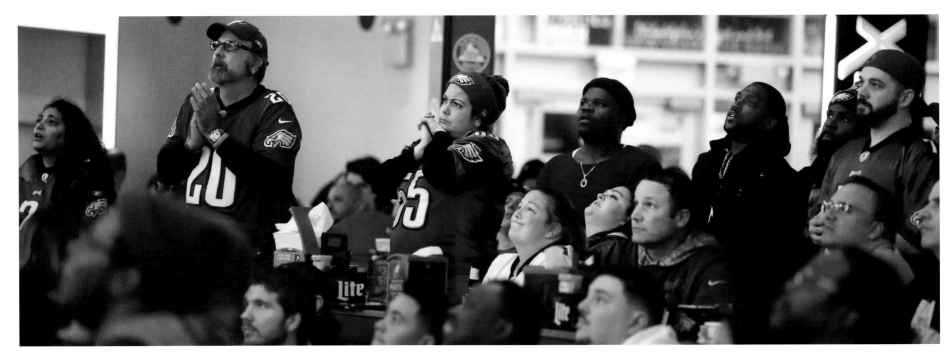

RIGHT: Tight end Trey Burton spikes the ball after catching his second touchdown pass of the game. From left, Nelson Agholor, Alshon Jeffery and Jay Ajayi join the celebration.

Yong Kim / Staff Photographer

ABOVE: Eagles fans cheer a fourth-quarter touchdown while they watch the game's telecast at XFINITY Live! in South Philadelphia. *Elizabeth Robertson / Staff Photographer*

LEFT: Defensive end Vinny Curry talks with Nick Foles after the victory in Los Angeles. *Yong Kim / Staff Photographer*

WRAPPING UP THE BYE

BY ZACH BERMAN / STAFF WRITER

EAST RUTHERFORD, N.J. — Once the Eagles had clinched a first-round bye, coach Doug Pederson shifted the focus away from the accomplishment and onto what it would take to be successful once they get there.

Pederson gathered his team after a suspenseful 34-29 win over the New York Giants to congratulate the Eagles on checking off another box among the team's goals before emphasizing that the way they played won't allow them to check off any boxes in January.

"Can't play like this and win in the postseason," Pederson said. "Got to come prepared. And when I say prepared, I think from a mental standpoint, that emotion, that sense of urgency, that dominating swagger that you want to see your team come out with."

Pederson's sentiment came after the Eagles advanced to 12-2. Nick Foles threw four touchdown passes in his first start replacing Carson Wentz. The biggest concern about the Eagles' postseason prospects might not be replacing Wentz but instead fixing a defense that allowed 504 yards to the lowly Giants, who entered the day averaging 208 fewer yards per game.

There was reason to be encouraged by Foles, who went 24 of 38 for 237 yards and no interceptions, although the Giants have the league's worst-ranked defense, so the effectiveness should not be a surprise.

The Eagles also benefited from the special teams, which blocked an extra point, a field goal, and a punt, all three of which were critical to the outcome. They took four points off the board, and the blocked punt set up an Eagles touchdown. In a close game, those plays mattered.

"We gave them a lot out there," linebacker Nigel Bradham said, referencing penalties and missed opportunities. "Stuff like that, when you play good teams—real good teams—it's going to put you in a bind to win a game."

Pederson was most vexed by the Giants converting 10 of 18 third downs—an outlier compared to their 33 percent conversion rate on third down entering the game,

OPPOSITE: Nigel Bradham wraps up running back Shane Vereen. *Yong Kim / Staff Photographer*

RIGHT: Eagles linebacker Kamu Grugier-Hill blocks a punt by New York's Brad Wing during the second quarter. *Yong Kim / Staff Photographer*

OPPOSITE LEFT: Nick Foles squeezes out a first down on a quarterback sneak in the fourth quarter. *David Maialetti / Staff Photographer*

OPPOSITE RIGHT: Alshon Jeffery hands the football to Nick Foles after Jeffery scored on a 3-yard pass. *David Maialetti / Staff Photographer*

and the 30.2 percent the Eagles have held opposing offenses to this season.

"That's your story right there," Pederson said.

Pleas for a better performance are easier to digest after a win, and the Eagles boarded their buses for a trip down the Jersey Turnpike with a first-round bye clinched and a chance to seal home-field advantage on Christmas.

"We still have everything right in front of us," Pederson said. "We have a great opportunity Christmas night to do some more and in the postseason."

TOTAL PLAYS

66
PHILADELPHIA

81
NEW YORK

"Can't play like this and win in the postseason."

— DOUG PEDERSON

RIGHT: Eagles cornerback Ronald Darby beats the Giants' Roger Lewis to the ball for an interception. *Yong Kim / Staff Photographer*

OPPOSITE: Malcolm Jenkins (center) blocks a field-goal attempt by New York's Aldrick Rosas in the fourth quarter. *David Maialetti / Staff Photographer*

Brandon Graham sacks Giants quarterback Eli Manning. *David Maialetti / Staff Photographer*

"We still have everything right in front of us."

— DOUG PEDERSON

LEFT: Malcolm Jenkins (left) and Corey Graham celebrate after the Eagles stopped the Giants on fourth down in the fourth quarter.

David Maialetti / Staff Photographer

RAIDING THE RAIDERS

BY JEFF MCLANE / STAFF WRITER

Ronald Darby had only played in front of the home Eagles fans once before Monday night. He hadn't known what it was like to win before the Lincoln Financial Field faithful in a game with playoff implications, let alone to be the hero.

But the cornerback went from goat to champion in a matter of a week — as quick as a Philadelphia minute during Eagles season. Darby's fourth-quarter, last-minute interception set up Jake Elliott's 48-yard game-winning field goal as the Eagles topped the feisty Raiders, 19-10, and clinched the No. 1 NFC seed.

For the second game in a row, Darby came up with a game-turning turnover. But his pick against the New York Giants was the lone positive on his ledger. He had what he said was one of the worst games of his career.

His performance, naturally, upset fans. But when he darted from the postgame locker room without answering questions and then began publicly blocking any of his critics on social media, some followers turned on Darby.

But he answered the music a few days later, apologizing for his actions, and that seemed to be enough for most. What mattered most was that Darby rebounded on the field and that the defense saved the day.

"I'm a good player this week, but any time down the road I'm going to be the worst player in the world again," Darby said. "That's just how it is. You've got to have a short memory."

On a night when Nick Foles and the offense struggled, Jim Schwartz's defense came up time and again in the second half. His unit forced four turnovers from the middle of the third quarter until Darby's pick — a Patrick Robinson interception, and Mychal Kendricks and Malcolm Jenkins forced fumbles before that.

Each one seemingly more important than the previous one. A last-second fumble by Raiders quarterback Derek Carr that Derek Barnett scooped for a score was the fifth.

"We needed all five to win the game," Jenkins said. "It was just one of those games when the defense needed to get stops for our offense.... It was the exact opposite of last week."

The lone Eagles TD on offense came on a 17-yard pass from Foles to Jay Ajayi.

OPPOSITE: After his fourth-quarter interception, Eagles cornerback Ronald Darby is flattened in celebration by teammate Jalen Mills. *Yong Kim / Staff Photographer*

"Coop's one of the hardest dudes in the league to get your hands on off the line."

— RONALD DARBY

Darby's interception came with just 54 seconds left. The Raiders faced second-and-10 on their 48. Carr, who had been confounded by the Eagles' pass defense for almost the entire night, dropped, surveyed the field, and threw to Amari Cooper.

But Darby jumped the route and secured the catch at the Eagles 48. Six plays later, Elliott kicked his second game-winner this season.

"Coop's one of the hardest dudes in the league to get your hands on off the line," Darby said. "When he started out slow, I just stayed square the whole time. And then when he made that step, boom, I just flipped and looked for the ball and I caught it."

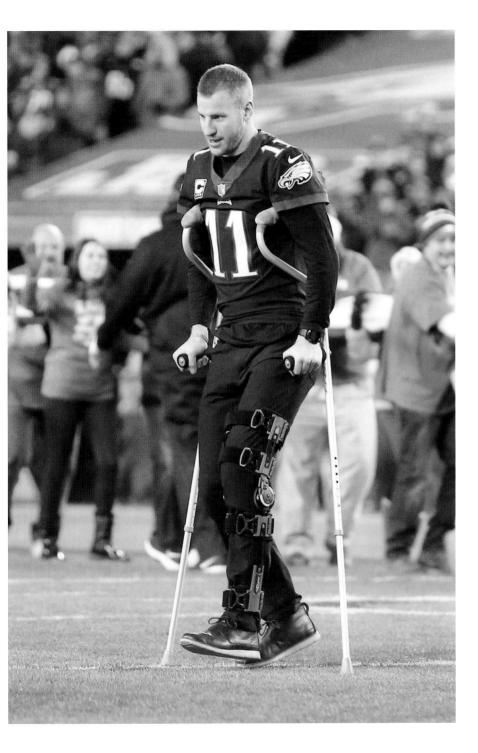

ABOVE: Flags fly outside Lincoln Financial Field before the Monday night game. *Jose F. Moreno / Staff Photographer*

LEFT: The injured Carson Wentz visits the field before the game. *Yong Kim / Staff Photographer*

OPPOSITE: Eagles wide receiver Mack Hollins gets into the spirit as he warms up for the Christmas night game. *Yong Kim / Staff Photographer*

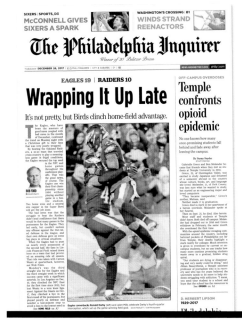

INQUIRER FRONT PAGE

TOP LEFT: Kenjon Barner escapes a diving tackle attempt by the Raiders' Nicholas Morrow on a punt return. *Yong Kim / Staff Photographer*

TOP FAR LEFT: Oakland's Jihad Ward sacks Nick Foles. The Eagles QB completed just 19 of 38 passes and was picked off once. *Dave Maialetti / Staff Photographer*

LEFT: Rookie Derek Barnett (96) walks off after scoring on a 23-yard fumble return on the game's final play. Jaylen Watkins (left) and Ronald Darby join him.
David Maialetti / Staff Photographer

OPPOSITE: Jay Ajayi launches into the end zone on a 17-yard pass from Nick Foles for the game's first score. Oakland's Karl Joseph (left) and Reggie Nelson pursue him. *Yong Kim / Staff Photographer*

CONCERN ABOUT THE QB

BY BOB FORD / SPORTS COLUMNIST

If it's any consolation for Eagles fans after watching the somewhat uninspiring performance of Nick Foles against the Cowboys, at least Carson Wentz's chances of winning the MVP award got a lot better.

We knew Wentz was good, and knew he lifted the whole team, but now it's clear exactly how much.

With their playoff seeding locked in place, the game against Dallas was supposed to be just a minor tune-up for the Eagles.

Well, the vehicle obviously needed more than a tune-up and, unfortunately, the part that is needed won't be available until next season. That's not the fault of Foles. He's a backup. He has to play only when something has gone terribly wrong. If the Eagles lose in the playoffs because Foles isn't as good as Wentz, that is simply the natural order of the NFL.

That said, hoo boy, he was bad.

It went beyond simply the stats, and those were bad enough in their own right. He completed just 4 of 11 attempts despite not being asked to convert very much aside from little swing passes and crossing patterns.

Foles played all four series of the first quarter before being lifted from the game, and he had the benefit of having the regulars out there with him with the exception of running back Jay Ajayi. The Eagles didn't convert any of the three third-down attempts in the quarter, which, combined with Christmas night against Oakland, makes Foles 1 of 17 on third-down tries in those two games.

But again, the numbers weren't the worst part. Foles just didn't seem comfortable, and teams can feel that about their quarterback the way a horse knows the difference between having a good jockey and a stable boy on its back.

Admittedly, it wasn't a day made for comfort. Game-time temperature was 18 degrees with a wind chill of 4 degrees. It was one of those days in which the ball can feel like a chunk of concrete in your hands.

"We as an offense expect to execute better. This wasn't acceptable," Foles said. "But we also know what we're capable of, and how talented we can be because of how we play together. We're going to keep our confidence high. There's no reason not to be confident."

We'll leave that one where it is for the moment. There are definitely a few reasons

---

OPPOSITE: Nick Foles pounces on his fumble during the first quarter. His outing was short and not fruitful. *Yong Kim / Staff Photographer*

RIGHT: A Nick Foles backer makes his feelings known in the stands at the Linc.
Clem Murray / Staff Photographer

for doubt among those outside the locker room. The team's job is to maintain an air of confidence regardless, and that will be the message for the next two weeks. The players saw Foles throw four touchdown passes against the Giants on Dec. 17 and they'll choose that memory over the fresher failures.

"The key is you remain confident because you know who you are.... We went out and played as hard as we could," Foles said. "We didn't execute, but that's stuff we can fix."

There are some things the Eagles can fix, and some things that, as said earlier, are beyond the healing ability of a tune-up.

There are things that will have to wait until next season.

For now, however, it will have to be dink, dunk, and defense that must carry the day. There is no other way, and the Eagles have to hope that formula holds together and that their opponents come apart.

Quarterback Nate Sudfeld chuckles as he realizes he went to the wrong side of the huddle during his first series against the Cowboys. *Clem Murray / Staff Photographer*

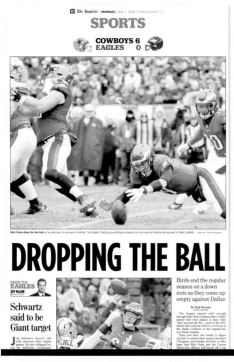

INQUIRER SPORTS PAGE

ABOVE RIGHT: Defensive end Vinny Curry (75) and safety Corey Graham celebrate after the Eagles stopped the Cowboys on fourth down. *Clem Murray / Staff Photographer*

RIGHT: On a frigid New Year's Eve, Eagles fans bundle up against the cold at Lincoln Financial Field. *Clem Murray / Staff Photographer*

OPPOSITE LEFT: Beau Allen loses his helmet while he finishes off a tackle of Cowboys running back Ezekiel Elliott. *Yong Kim / Staff Photographer*

OPPOSITE RIGHT: Whoops: Just before a punt, Donnie Jones removes his warm-up pants, which he mistakenly wore onto the field. *Yong Kim / Staff Photographer*

BIG FINISH BY DEFENSE

BY BOB FORD / COLUMNIST

If the expectation going into the divisional round playoff game was that the Eagles' defense would need to carry the day against the Atlanta Falcons, holding down the score while its own offense produced what meager amount it could, that expectation became the reality by the end of the afternoon.

Retrospect changes everything, of course, but if the task had been put that bluntly — the Falcons must be limited to no more than 14 points — the likelihood of hosting the National Football Conference championship game wouldn't have seemed likely at all.

"That's crazy. That last drive was crazy," linebacker Mychal Kendricks said after the 15-10 victory at Lincoln Financial Field. "But we've been there before this season.

We know what it takes to win the big game. It comes down to who has the ball last, and who wants it more."

Kendricks was still bouncing around the locker room, still in his uniform, just minutes removed from the play that decided the game, a fourth-and-goal from the 2-yard line, with Atlanta quarterback Matt Ryan eventually settling for a prayer to Julio Jones that wasn't answered.

The truth is that the defense hadn't been in that situation during the regular season — not even close. It forced Carolina to punt from around midfield as the Eagles held a five-point lead in the closing minutes of that game, and it forced a punt from the Rams, holding a two-point lead, with about two minutes to play. But that was as close to what the Eagles faced in this game as it

got, and that isn't very close.

Ryan had taken the Falcons from their own 24-yard line, survived one fourth-down conversion, and gotten his team in position to take four makeable shots into the end zone for the win. Not just any win, but a win that would extend one team's season and end another's.

So, no, the Eagles hadn't been there before. Their preparation throughout the season is what got them through when the challenge did rise up before them.

"Watch this, watch this," Kendricks said, grabbing fellow linebacker Nigel Bradham in the next locker. "Y-off, 3-by-1. What's coming?"

"Sprint out," Bradham said.

"Y-off, 3-by-1. We all knew what was coming," Kendricks said, hooking a thumb

---

OPPOSITE: Nigel Bradham (left) and Brandon Graham sack Atlanta's Matt Ryan during the third quarter. *David Maialetti / Staff Photographer*

TOTAL YARDS

334
PHILADELPHIA

281
ATLANTA

"Obviously, the whole season was on that play right there."

— MALCOLM JENKINS

toward Bradham. "And he rushed the quarterback and made him hurry."

On that deciding fourth down, Ryan did sprint out to the right, just as Kendricks and Bradham knew was coming, just as safety Malcolm Jenkins called out to the rest of the defensive backfield. The Eagles flowed that way, double-covering the slot receiver and tying up the tight end with pressure around that end. That left just Jones along the sideline in the end zone and a jump ball with Jalen Mills that Ryan sent their way just before Bradham reached him.

"Obviously, the whole season was on that play right there," Jenkins said. "We were pretty confident they'd move the pocket on that type of play. We recognized the formation as soon as they lined up and were able to take away the first two reads on the sprint out, and he tossed it up into coverage, and we move on."

ABOVE: Alshon Jeffery outruns Atlanta's Robert Alford down the sideline on a 21-yard pass play. *Michael Bryant / Staff Photographer*

LEFT: Eagles cornerbacks Jalen Mills (left) and Ronald Darby celebrate a third-quarter stop. *Yong Kim / Staff Photographer*

OPPOSITE: Eagles running back Jay Ajayi crashes down after a hit by Brooks Reed. *Yong Kim / Staff Photographer*

DAILY NEWS FRONT PAGE

ABOVE LEFT: LeGarrette Blount outruns Falcons linebacker Kemal Ishmael for an Eagles touchdown in the second quarter. *Tim Tai / Staff Photographer*

LEFT: Jake Elliott kicks one of his two field goals in the second half. *Tim Tai / Staff Photographer*

FAR LEFT: Fans cheer for their underdog Eagles during the second half at the Linc. *Tim Tai / Staff Photographer*

OPPOSITE: Fans at the Linc revel in their underdog team's victory. *Elizabeth Robertson / Staff Photographer*

ABOVE: Mychal Kendricks (obscured) tackles Atlanta's Devonta Freeman for a loss as Rodney McLeod (23) moves in. *Michael Bryant / Staff Photographer*

LEFT: Falcons receiver Julio Jones cannot come up with a catch in the end zone on the game's final play, thanks to tight coverage by Jalen Mills. *Yong Kim / Staff Photographer*

OPPOSITE: Fans at the Linc go wild with the Eagles leading in the fourth quarter. *David Maialetti / Staff Photographer*

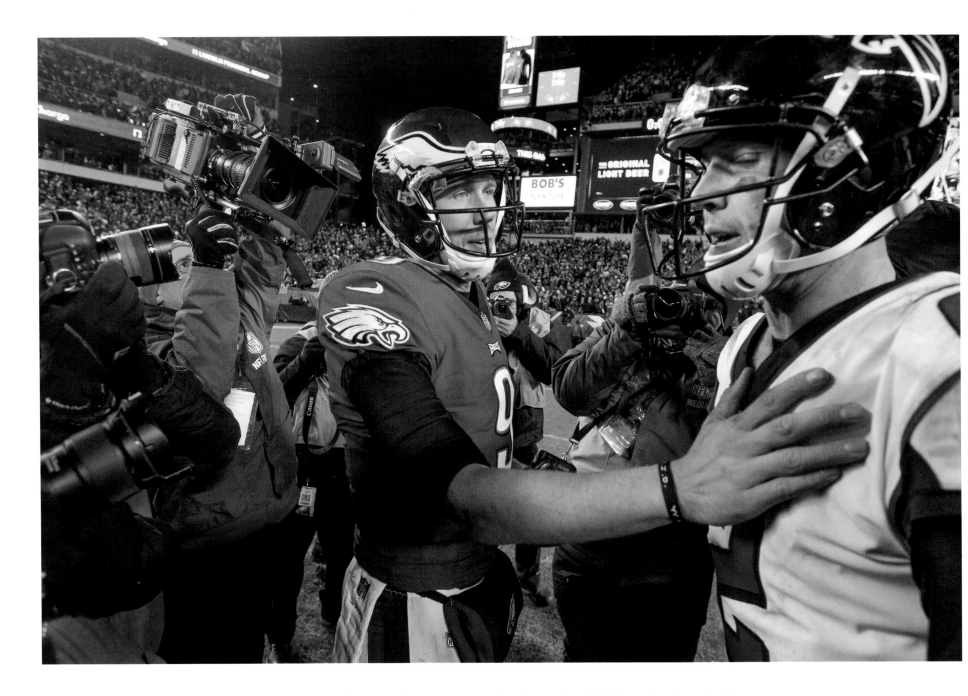

The quarterbacks talk after Nick Foles and the Eagles knocked off Matt Ryan (right) and the Falcons. *Michael Bryant / Staff Photographer*

Tackle Lane Johnson wears a dog mask, and starts a Philly fad, after the underdog Eagles beat the Falcons. *Michael Bryant / Staff Photographer*

A BLOWOUT AND A BLAST

BY MIKE SIELSKI / COLUMNIST

The biggest, loudest sports party that Philadelphia had thrown in nearly a decade looked and sounded like this: people wearing green shirts and dog masks screaming and whooping until their lungs burned and the building shook, a journeyman defensive back intercepting a pass and weaving from one side of the field to the other before slipping into the end zone and dashing down a tunnel, a head coach calling daring plays without fear against the best defense in the National Football League, a backup quarterback flinging deep passes to wide-open receivers and threading passes to less-open ones, a city that has never celebrated a Super Bowl victory now alive and thrumming with what might yet be.

Let's get the barest of facts out of the way first, because the rest of the night requires more thought, and perhaps a good stiff drink, to process. The Eagles beat the Minnesota Vikings, 38-7, at Lincoln Financial Field in the NFC championship game. On Feb. 4, at U.S. Bank Stadium in Minneapolis, they will play the New England Patriots — the sport's preeminent dynasty of the 21st century, with the sport's preeminent coach, Bill Belichick, and the sport's preeminent quarterback, Tom Brady — in Super Bowl LII. This is just the third time that the Eagles have reached the Super Bowl and the first time since 2005, when they lost to ... the Patriots. They have never won one.

Doug Pederson, the head coach whom the Eagles had all but settled on two years ago, was two steps ahead of Vikings coach Mike Zimmer all game. Instead of relying on a conservative game plan, Pederson called plays as if Carson Wentz had not torn the anterior cruciate ligament in his left knee last month, as if he were still the Eagles' quarterback and not Nick Foles. Pederson had Foles throw early, often, and down the field, and when Foles did, he often found his receivers — Alshon Jeffery, Torrey Smith, Zach Ertz — without a Vikings player near them.

"The message is still the same: Go be Nick," Pederson had said Friday. "Feed off of last week, obviously. Different set of challenges, different team, different defense and all that. Don't have to force

---

OPPOSITE: Eagles guard Stefen Wisniewski pulls off a Linc Leap into the crowd after Alshon Jeffery's fourth-quarter touchdown. *David Maialetti / Staff Photographer*

RIGHT: Toasting the Eagles in dog masks, fans (from left) Adam Gatsis, Nick Paris and Mike Stergion tailgate before the game. *Jose F. Moreno / Staff Photographer*

OPPOSITE: Vikings linebacker Eric Kendricks goes airborne as he tries to tackle Jay Ajayi. *Tim Tai / Staff Photographer*

anything. Just let the offense work for you, and he'll be fine."

Foles had been solid in the Eagles' divisional-round victory over the Atlanta Falcons, but he was spectacular against the Vikings, completing 26 of his 33 passes for 352 yards and three touchdowns. Beyond the mere statistics, though, he played with a comfort that belied the manner in which he had performed in the regular season's final two games. He had appeared unsure of himself then, tentative when he threw. It was natural to believe that, because Wentz was on his way to being named the league's most valuable player, because Wentz was so breathtaking and important a player, the Eagles wouldn't just be vulnerable without him — they would be a sickly approximation of the team they had been with him. Somehow, though, Wentz's injury fortified them, Foles most of all.

DAILY NEWS FRONT PAGE

RIGHT: Derek Barnett strips Vikings quarterback Case Keenum of the football in the second quarter.
Yong Kim / Staff Photographer

OPPOSITE: Lara Diukina celebrates a touchdown during the second quarter of the NFC championship game.
Tim Tai / Staff Photographer

RIGHT: Nick Foles celebrates his 53-yard touchdown pass to Alshon Jeffery.
Yong Kim / Staff Photographer

OPPOSITE: Torrey Smith hauls in a 41-yard TD pass on a flea-flicker from Nick Foles. Harrison Smith of the Vikings arrives too late.
Michael Bryant / Staff Photographer

ABOVE: Eagles executive Howie Roseman (left) rejoices with coach Doug Pederson at the end of the game. *Michael Bryant / Staff Photographer*

RIGHT: Alshon Jeffery streaks into the end zone on a 53-yard pass to give the Eagles a 21-7 advantage. *Michael Bryant / Staff Photographer*

OPPOSITE: Team owner Jeffrey Lurie dances with Eagles players on the field to celebrate their NFC championship. *Yong Kim / Staff Photographer*

Eagles owner Jeffrey Lurie holds up the George Halas Trophy as coach Doug Pederson applauds.

David Maialetti / Staff Photographer

Eagles fans take to the streets at Broad and Walnut to revel in the team's victory in the NFC championship game.

Tom Gralish / Staff Photographer

FLYING HIGH NOW

BY ZACH BERMAN / STAFF WRITER

MINNEAPOLIS — This night will be remembered for decades in Philadelphia, when old friends reminisce about where they were on Feb. 4, 2018, and parents tell their children about the moment the Eagles won their first Super Bowl. They'll remember when Doug Pederson called the trick play at the goal line, when Zach Ertz dove into the end zone in the fourth quarter, when Brandon Graham stripped Tom Brady of the ball, and when the greatest dynasty in NFL history fell to an improbable champion from Philadelphia.

The Eagles won the Super Bowl. You can read that again. It's not going away. The Eagles beat the New England Patriots, 41-33, at U.S. Bank Stadium to hoist the Lombardi Trophy for the first time in franchise history. A team with a backup quarterback and with players who wore underdog masks throughout the playoffs because they were never favored to win sent Brady and Bill Belichick home with a Super Bowl loss.

Pederson gathered his team together in the postgame locker room after the players danced and sang and chewed cigars and sipped scotch and enjoyed a euphoria that can only be experienced after winning a Super Bowl. He recited what had become a mantra for the team.

"An individual can make a difference," Pederson told the Eagles, "but a team makes a miracle!"

It was one of the best Super Bowls ever played, and it had a finish that befit this year's Eagles. When Nick Foles connected with Ertz for a go-ahead touchdown with 2 minutes, 21 seconds remaining to give the Eagles a five-point edge, the excitement of the fourth-quarter lead collided with the anxiety prompted by knowing Brady was on the other sideline. The greatest quarterback in NFL history took the ball with a chance to win — and the Eagles didn't let him. Graham pushed through the Patriots' offensive line and drove Brady down, popping the ball loose. Rookie Derek Barnett recovered the fumble.

A late field goal by Jake Elliott gave the Eagles an eight-point lead and Brady had no magic left.

"It hasn't really sunk in, but I'm so excited for that locker room," Pederson said. "Everything that we've been through this season, to get to this point — a lot of people counted us out — but that locker room believed, believed in each other, believed in me. ... We found a way to get it done."

OPPOSITE: Eagles coach Doug Pederson shares the moment with his quarterback, Super Bowl MVP Nick Foles. *Yong Kim / Staff Photographer*

INQUIRER SUPER BOWL PREVIEW

RIGHT: Zach Ertz (86) and Fletcher Cox lead the Eagles onto the field before the start of Super Bowl LII.

Michael Bryant / Staff Photographer

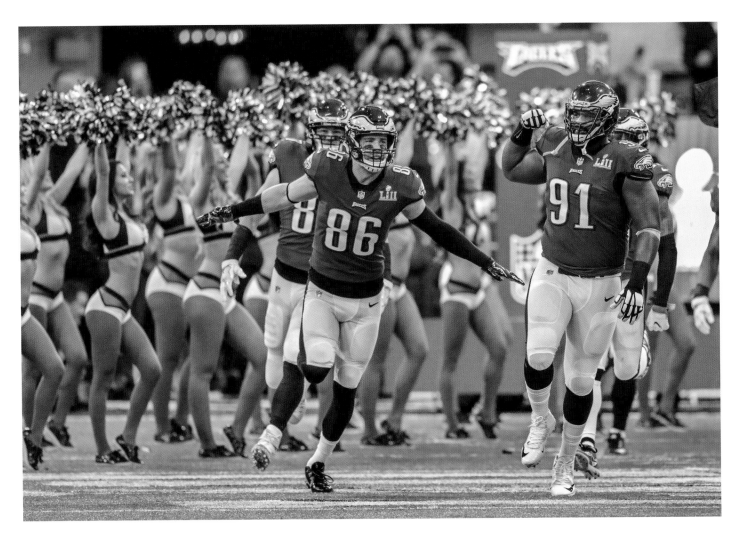

This moment is bigger than what happened during 60 minutes on Feb. 4. Try nearly 60 years, generations of Eagles fans waiting since 1960 for this type of celebration. There were all those autumn Sundays, from the Franklin Field bleachers to the 700 Level at Veterans Stadium to pristine Lincoln Financial Field. There were seasons that started with championship promise and all finished with the bitter disappointment of the city's desire going unfulfilled. And it would renew each year, from the draft to training camp to the preseason into the regular season, with every weekend serving as a referendum and the Monday-morning mood throughout the region dictated by the final score the day before. If the fans were lucky, they had postseason football. But the last game was never a victory.

Not this year. Not these Eagles.

Foles finished 28 of 43 for 373 yards with three passing touchdowns and one receiving touchdown. He was named MVP of the game.

"I think the big thing that helped me was knowing that I didn't have to be Superman," Foles said. "I have amazing teammates, amazing coaches around me."

TOTAL YARDS

538
PHILADELPHIA

613
NEW ENGLAND

"An individual can make a difference, but a team makes a miracle!"

— DOUG PEDERSON

LEFT: New England receiver Brandin Cooks is tackled by Rodney McLeod during the first half. *Tim Tai / Staff Photographer*

ABOVE: Harrison Buck lets out a cheer as the Eagles close the book on the Patriots in Super Bowl LII.
David Swanson / Staff Photographer

RIGHT: Alshon Jeffery pulls in a 34-yard touchdown pass from Nick Foles above Patriots cornerback Eric Rowe.
Michael Bryant / Staff Photographer

OPPOSITE: Eagles safety Malcolm Jenkins knocks New England's Brandin Cooks out of the game with a jarring hit. *David Maialetti / Staff Photographer*

Running back LeGarrette Blount lands in the end zone over the Patriots' Duron Harmon for an Eagles touchdown in the second quarter. *Yong Kim / Staff Photographer*

Eagles rookie Corey Clement fights off New England's Duron Harmon during his 55-yard reception in the second quarter.

Michael Bryant / Staff Photographer

ABOVE: Nick Foles runs untouched into the end zone on a trick play, a pass from Trey Burton. *Michael Bryant / Staff Photographer*

RIGHT: He can catch, too: Foles (9) and his teammates go wild after the quarterback scored on a pass from tight end Burton with 34 seconds left in the first half. The Eagles pulled off the trick play on fourth down. *David Swanson / Staff Photographer*

OPPOSITE: Nick Foles celebrates his remarkable touchdown catch with backup quarterback Nate Sudfeld.
Yong Kim / Staff Photographer

Cory Clement catches a 22-yard TD pass from Nick Foles ahead of New England's Marquis Flowers and Devin McCourty (32). *Michael Bryant / Staff Photographer*

Zach Ertz dives over New England's Devin McCourty to score the go-ahead touchdown in the fourth quarter.

David Maialetti / Staff Photographer

INQUIRER FRONT PAGE

ABOVE LEFT: At Chickie's and Pete's in South Philadelphia, Eagles fans rejoice after a touchdown. *Elizabeth Robertson / Staff Photographer*

ABOVE FAR LEFT: Phil DiTullio and his father, Robert, let their emotions flow after Brandon Graham's crucial defensive play late in the game. The pair watched the Super Bowl at XFINITY Live! near the Linc. *Charles Fox / Staff Photographer*

LEFT: Fans watching the game at XFINITY Live! in South Philadelphia exult as the clock expires on the Patriots. *Charles Fox / Staff Photographer*

OPPOSITE: Eagles defensive end Brandon Graham knocks the ball out of Tom Brady's hand on a crucial fourth-quarter play. Derek Barnett recovered the fumble. *David Maialetti / Staff Photographer*

On the Super Bowl's final play, Patriots tight end Rob Gronkowski cannot come up with
a desperation pass from Tom Brady as Eagles swarm around him.

Steven M. Falk / Staff Photographer

Eagles running back Jay Ajayi reflects on the Super Bowl triumph on the confetti-covered field at U.S. Bank Stadium.

David Maialetti / Staff Photographer

RIGHT: Eagles Beau Allen (left), Brent Celek (center) and Jason Kelce soak up that winning feeling on the field in Minneapolis.
Michael Bryant / Staff Photographer

BELOW RIGHT: Tom Brady leaves the field after the loss. The Patriots quarterback passed for 505 yards and three touchdowns.
Tim Tai / Staff Photographer

BELOW: Coach Doug Pederson and Eagles owner Jeffrey Lurie (center) rejoice as they wait with Nick Foles to receive the Lombardi Trophy.
Michael Bryant / Staff Photographer

Defensive hero Brandon Graham shares his trophy moment with his wife, Carlyne, and daughter, Emerson Abigail.

Michael Bryant / Staff Photographer

ABOVE RIGHT: The Super Bowl party spills into the streets as fans flock to Cottman and Frankford Avenues in the city's Mayfair section.
Joseph Kaczmarek / for The Inquirer

BELOW RIGHT: On Temple's campus near Broad Street and Cecil B. Moore Avenue, police officers and joyous Eagles fans react at the end of the game.
Mark C. Psoras / for The Inquirer

OPPOSITE: With City Hall as a backdrop, Eagles followers keep the party going near Broad and Walnut Streets after the Super Bowl.
Tom Gralish / Staff Photographer

The Eagles' mascot, Swoop, stands at the front of the truck as the Super Bowl
champions parade up Broad Street. *Tom Gralish / Staff Photographer*

ABOVE: Eagles fans in South Philadelphia watch their heroes from the top of a school building on Broad Street. *Jose F. Moreno / Staff Photographer*

BELOW: Parade viewers perch on city garbage trucks to get a better view at Broad and Arch Streets. *Michael Bryant / Staff Photographer*

ABOVE: Revelers climb a statue on Broad Street after the Eagles parade went around City Hall. *Tom Gralish / Staff Photographer*

BELOW: A statue near City Hall becomes a seat for fans as the Eagles pass by. *Tim Tai / Staff Photographer*

ABOVE: On JFK Boulevard across from Dilworth Plaza, a shelter for SEPTA passengers becomes parade seating for some fans. *Michael Bryant / Staff Photographer*

BELOW: A fan sprays a fire extinguisher from atop a light pole as the parade for the Super Bowl champions reaches the Art Museum. *David Maialetti / Staff Photographer*

With City Hall in the background, Eagles quarterbacks (from left) Nick Foles, Nate Sudfeld and Carson Wentz show off the Vince Lombardi Trophy aboard their bus. At left is Eagles owner Jeffrey Lurie. *Michael Bryant / Staff Photographer*

Fans are packed in on the Benjamin Franklin Parkway as the Eagles conclude their day of celebration at the Art Museum. *David Maialetti / Staff Photographer*

A massive crowd of fans fills Eakins Oval as the Eagles finish the day's celebration on the Art Museum steps.

Jessica Griffin / Staff Photographer

LEFT: Eagles players soak up the cheers as they ride past the huge crowd near City Hall.
Michael Bryant / Staff Photographer

FAR LEFT: Eagles cornerback Jalen Mills takes a break from the bus to mingle with the crowd along South Broad Street.
Steven M. Falk / Staff Photographer

BELOW: Dressed in Mummers attire, Eagles center Jason Kelce pauses during his colorful speech on the Art Museum steps. *David Maialetti / Staff Photographer*

SUPPORTING PARTNERS

Philly proud.

When you were underdogs, Philly believed. When you took chances, Philly had faith. When you became champions, Philly roared. Congratulations to the Eagles, from a city of proud fans.